COPYCAT

COPYCAT
and a litter of other cats

a very important book by **David Yow**

AKASHIC BOOKS

Published by Akashic Books
©2014 by David Yow

ISBN-13: 978-1-61775-270-4
Library of Congress Control Number: 2013956775

Printed in China
First printing

Akashic Books
PO Box 1456
New York, NY 10009
info@akashicbooks.com
www.akashicbooks.com

for Little Buddy, Penny, and Nico

and Me Yow, Spunky, Miss M, Boo,
Honey, Precious, Hugh, Space
Monkey, David, Algernon, Grady,
and Rizz Rizz Rizz

Thank you:
Ellen Philips
Derek Larson
Rob Rowe and Rhonda Reynolds
Julia Rose Brown
Josh Siegel
Bruce A. Hornstein, OD

A very long time ago in Austin, Texas, I became friends with a fella goes by the name of Tom (that's Mr. van den Bout to you). He and I had a lovely time. On one particularly sunny afternoon I had my doodle pad out and I was doodlin'. I depicted something of a cartoon cat standing there just lookin' straight at ya. I put a little T-shirt on the pussycat and scribbled the name *Tom* on the front of the shirt. Makes perfect sense that I would entitle this artwork *Tomcat.* Tom was courting a delightful young lady who was known as Cheryl (that's Miss Bostick to you). I designed a very similar feline to what I had done with *Tomcat*, but made it slightly different by scrawling the name *Cheryl* on the front of the animal's garment. I gave that drawing the name *Cheryl Cat.* This foolishness led me to draw a whole litter of cats, most of which have a comical twist or a punlike idea accompanying them. The inventory grew to a number in excess of ninety. The only criterion for each cartoon was that its title contain the letters C, A, and T, in that order. I trust you to be a clever and enterprising individual, elsewise you would not be regarding this book. So please feel free to pat yourself on the back when you think up titles that I have not included herein.

David Yow

(*Cheryl Cat* did not make the grade.)

In no particular order . . .

Catatonic

13

Alley Cat

Bobcat

17

Catheter

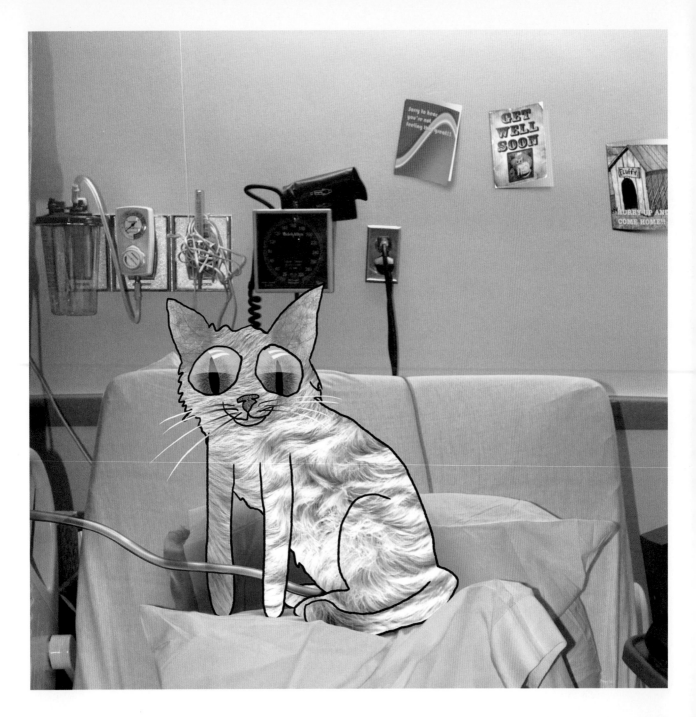

Catholic

Domestic Cat

Cat on a Hot Tin Roof

Catcall

Catsup

Cattails

Catalina

Catastrophe

Polecat

Grumpy Cat

Felix the Cat

Cat Carrier

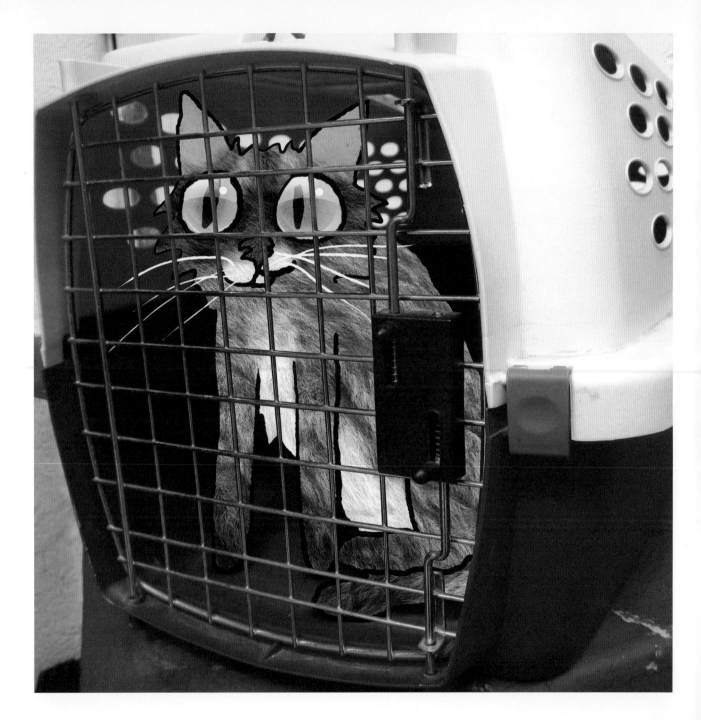

Cat Ballou

Catbird

Catalyst

Cat's Cradle

Tabby Cat

Stray Cat

Catwalk

Cattle

Catnip

Catnap

Catfight

Caterpillar

Catwoman

Sylvester the Cat

Tomcat

Cattywampus

Catskills

Cat

Catlike

Fat Cat

Top Cat

Cat and Mouse

Cat's Pajamas

Stimpson J. Cat

Black Cat

Scat

Category

Catfish

Cat Litter

Cathouse

Catalog

Catalog
August 2, 1906
Leland, Oregon

105

Big Cat

Cat Burglar

Copycat

CAT Scan

Catty-Corner

Catacomb

Cool Cat

Cataract

Scaredy-Cat

Wildcat

Cat-o'-Nine-Tails

Cat Got Your Tongue?

Catamaran

Cat Box

Cat's Meow

Cat in the Hat

Cat Stevens

Catgut

Catapult

Catharsis

Cat Scratch Fever

Catsuit

Cat Power

Cate Blanchett

Catalytic Converter

Caterer

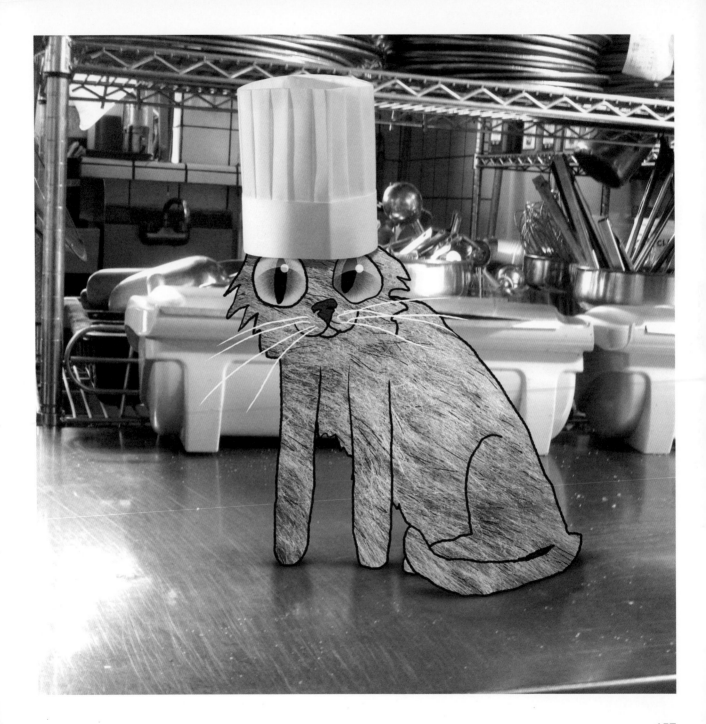

Index